Business Networking

31 Ways To Start Conversations And End Conversations To Make Sure You Gather Contact Info And Keep In Touch

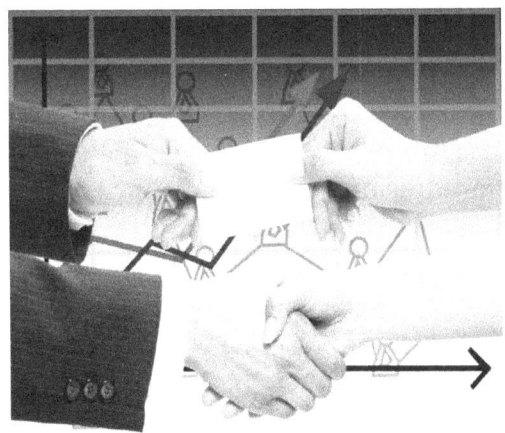

By

Fhilcar Faunillan

The information provided herein is stated to be truthful and consistent, in that any liability, in terms of inattention or otherwise, by any usage or abuse of any policies, processes, or directions contained within is the solitary and utter responsibility of the recipient reader. Under no circumstances will any legal responsibility or blame be held against the publisher for any damages, reparation, or monetary loss due to the information herein, either directly or indirectly.

All copyrights not held by the publisher are retained by their respective authors.

The information herein is offered for informational purposes solely, and is universal as so. The presentation of the information is without contract or any type of guarantee assurance.

Where trademarks are used without any consent, it can be understood that the said publication of the trademark is without prior backing or permission by its trademark owner. All trademarks and brands within this book are for clarifying purposes only and are the owned by the owners themselves, not affiliated with this document.

Table of Contents

INTRODUCTION

I want to thank you and congratulate you for downloading the book, *"Business Networking: 31 Ways to Start Conversations and End Conversations to Make Sure You Gather Contact Info and Keep in Touch"*.

This book contains proven steps and strategies on how to build and broaden your business network by giving you the basic conversations for a successful transaction.

You're at an event picking your way through your food and watching as other people are huddled together, sharing some jokes and conversations. The seat has been warmed up enough and getting out of it would be the best idea of the century for the next few minutes. You want to strike up a conversation because it's what you're there for but no. Not a single word comes out. Your voice box is alright and you can speak the English language. But you've seem to have forgotten how to string up sentences.

You try to approach a person and the only thing that comes out of your mouth is, "Um." Talk about embarrassment!

As a person involved in business networking, this is seriously not the way your day should be going. You need to actually be talking to people so you can build a business relationship with them and mouthing mono-syllabic words would hardly help.

This book will give you 31 ways to start and end conversations to ensure that you will not go home empty-handed. These liners would guarantee that you get to keep the contact information of the people you'll meet and be able to keep in touch with them.

This book will also guide you through the things you need to observe before and during talking to a potential business contact.

Thanks again for downloading this book, I hope you enjoy it!

Chapter 1 - The Way Business Networking Is Handled

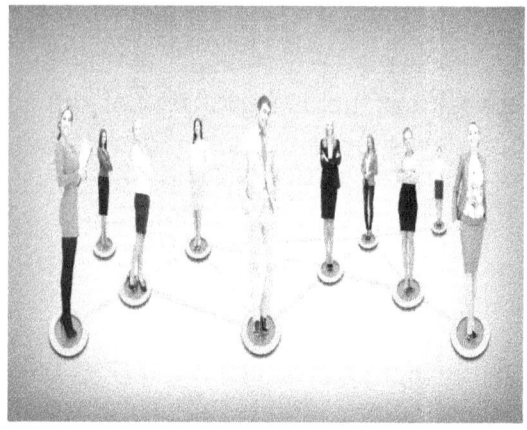

Ever heard of the term business networking? Does it sound like getting dealers of your products or services or is it a sort of a membership program like that of Avon? What is its significance in your business and profession?

Business networking is a marketing method whose objective is to gain sales opportunities and build up contacts. It is generally a low cost way that relies heavily on introductions and referrals which one can do through personal and face-to-face meetings, email, phone, and social networking sites.

Those doing business have claimed that business networking is very ideal because it's more cost-effective compared to the other kinds or methods of business generation. Advertising through whatever media be it print, radio, or television for example, takes up a lot of manpower to produce ads and most importantly, money in order to distribute and reproduce them. Depending on the media you are going to use, advertising cost would vary. Say for instance, in print (magazines or newspapers), size, section where your ad appears, scope of publication, and a lot more are the basis for pricing. For broadcasted ads, the timeslot, length or duration are among the things that affect the ad's cost. Instead of money, business networking, on the other hand, has the people's dedication and personal commitment as its backbone.

Another advantage that business networking has over advertising is its more intimate approach towards attracting potential clients. Ads feel so impersonal, like they couldn't care less if you entertain their products and ideas or not. However, when someone approaches you and takes the effort and time to talk to you, it goes a long way in making you feel attended to and special. The moment you begin to talk, you build a personal connection with your receiver and the probable ratio is 1:1.

Furthermore, taking up business networking does not demand superior technical skills. Take note, it is all about the connections. And it is not about what you know but *who* you know.

Many of the principles that you must embrace and behaviors that you should observe are easy to grasp as they are practically of common sense. What do you do in normal business transactions? Let us see, what do you do in relationships? How do you start one? You talk.

Without communication, there can be no relationship. You cannot establish one. Remember the times when you've had world wars with your life partners because you do not talk enough or you said something wrong or you talk too much or you do not talk right. Talking is the key activity, ladies and gentlemen. Forget about other kinds of activities that you know. In business networking, if you don't open your mouth, then you are certainly out.

Talking is just the way to get contact information from potential business associates. And talking is the way to attracting their interest enough so that you can have a higher chance that they will keep in touch with you afterwards.

Chapter 2 - The Way You Should Treat Conversation Starters And Enders

Imagine a person you meet for the first time and one starts by asking you, "Are you single?" Of course, if you are in a bar or a place to party on a weekend, then that would be appropriate and relevant. But if you are in a business event, how about you just go wish for a sinkhole to eat you up?

The strategy to amassing contacts at the end of the day is treating conversation starters and enders as very important matters that you should pay with utmost attention. Normally, we do not put up much thought about how we approach someone and initiate conversations with them. Normally, we do not even put in effort to talk at all. It is palpable that you can't apply these scenarios when you are doing business networking.

What you say to a person the first time you meet them may not always be remembered but the impression you leave will. Start talking to someone by calling them by some offensive name in a really hostile tone and your image as a douchebag will certainly be cemented. Since business networking depends on the business relationships with other people that you can establish, it is important to be able to get people to talk to you, enough that they will feel comfortable to leave you with their contact information and respond to any attempts at communication in the future. You should remember that the first thing to do is for you to build an impression and once it has been rooted in your prospect's mind, you are one step closer to your aim.

You should give the same amount of attention when you end your conversations with potential business contacts. Saying these lines: "Okay, bye" or "Okay, I'm going to go", or "Thanks, bye" will only not come off as offensive but they will also affect any kind of positive vibe you have given off during your conversation with the person.

There are those who are very good at starting conversations but forget to do well in ending them because they thought they have already achieved their goals beforehand. Remember that contact information may be on your hands but if you could not keep in touch with them, then you have just wasted your time. And you know what could jeopardize your chances? Well, it is a really lame parting remark.

Chapter 3 - Ways Which You Should And Shouldn't Do Before Talking

Do not ever think being crass is endearing.

Keep in mind that it is a business meeting that you are attending, not a bar. Heck, even in bars, being rude and obnoxious is not at all charming. Keep your attitude in check. Be reminded that business networking requires people skills. And being obtuse is not part of the description.

Get a feeling on the kind of person you are talking to.

Let your instincts run free and get a feel of the person whom you are planning to approach. If you think that he or she the kind of person who will not enjoy small talks, then don't do it. Forget it! Also, observe and be careful in choosing people with whom you are willing to say jokes to. You might be offending or insulting someone even without you knowing.

Smile.

Do not act like you are on your own version of Torture Reality. You do not always have to initiate conversations all the time. You can lay low for a while. But while you are doing this, do not just stand in the corner with your arms crossed in front of your chest, sulking and irritable. This will definitely discourage anyone from approaching you. Look warm and open so others will also think to approach you.

Do not make assumptions regarding very personal topics.

Do not ask how his wife is doing. Why is that so? Simple. You are not even sure if he is married or if he even swings that way. These kinds of questions could also be a source of discomfort if they would hit a nerve and will stale the conversation. In short, it is quite awkward. Even asking about the university they went to is pretty unsafe. Some of the people you will meet would not probably have the same level of educational attainment as yours. As a result, you will just end up being uncomfortable.

Be Present.

When you are talking to someone, keep in mind that you need to pay attention to whom you are with. Do not worry too much about what you have to say next and just speak your thoughts. Furthermore, to show that your mind has not wandered, you can make comments on the ideas shared and follow them up with questions.

Dress appropriately.

Make sure to do your homework on the kind of dress code required during the event. Usually, business networking meet-ups would welcome business professional get-ups.

Be equipped.

Bring your updated business card and keep perhaps a paper and pen where you can write down contact information of people you will be talking to. If you have a mini journal, then you can include that there and simply update later on.

Mind your body language and attitude.

Nonverbal cues and body language can be used to communicate with others. When you are talking to someone, make sure that you are not giving off "I'm bored" or "I'm not at all interested" vibes. That will make the other person feel really bad.

Remember names.

This may be hard for others but remembering the names of the people you have talked to will be helpful. During conversations, recalling and mentioning their names (e.g. when you say goodbye) will have a positive effect on their impression of you because it goes to show that you are really interested in the conversation. Giving them a feeling of importance is likewise manifested here and that would translate to a special treatment on the other person's part.

Chapter 4 - 31 Ways To Start Conversations

Alright then, now you have learned what business networking is and its relevance to you in gaining connections in order to hit that one big deal. So we come back to our problem. In any other day, you're a normal human being with the speech capabilities fit for your age. You are plainly normal and is a good conversant whenever you are with your family and friends. You love to share and give your opinion and the likes. But when it comes to striking up a conversation in a setting where you have to bear in mind that the people you have to talk to must not end up running the other way, well that is a whole different story.

You don't have to worry at all. This is a common problem that networkers face. How exactly do you just approach someone, intrude into their personal space, and start talking? Actually, it is not as scary as you think. Take that first step and do not be afraid to talk. Other people in the room will actually feel relieved that you took the initiative and initiated a conversation first. Trust me; no one is going to snub you because you share the same goal of establishing contact with others.

So here are 31 ways to start your conversations. Open that mouth and keep the words coming!

Saying Hello #1: *"Hi."*

Saying Hello #2: *"Hey, I'm Naomi."*

Saying Hello #3: *"I don't really know a lot of people here so I just came to say hello. I'm Joe."*

It will not hurt to start your conversations the usual way. If you are not the kind of person who can deliver complicated lines or if you are too nervous to try to muster the courage to speak more than 5 words in a row, then you can decide for the easy openers. You can also add a little handshake whenever you introduce yourself.

Saying Hello #4: *"Do you know what this dish is made of?"*

Saying Hello #5: *"Oh, thank God. They have sushi. Have you tried this before?"*

Saying Hello #6: *"Do you know how to cook this? It tastes awesome."*

The food table is not just for eating. It can also be your hunting ground. You can approach the people who are hovering over the food because I bet you they are not just lingering for the food but also for the chance to get to talk to someone. Furthermore, the very food in front of you can be your topic or subject matter so you won't need to rack up and turn your mind upside down looking for a decent topic.

Saying Hello #7: *"It is so warm in here."*

Saying Hello #8: *"This is a wonderful place. Is this your first time here?"*

Saying Hello #9: *"Have you seen the painting by the fireplace? It looks terrible, right?"*

No matter what the differences are, it is a fact that you will always share a common ground with the people in the room. You will surely notice that when you will get used to attending talks or expanding your network in the future. You may be coming from different companies but you share the same space right now and you can find inspiration from your surroundings on what to say at the beginning of your conversation. You can talk about the ambience in the room, the grandeur of the place the event is held, or even about the traffic you experienced on the way.

Do not be afraid to voice out your opinions about something you noticed in the venue. As long as you say it with an appropriate tone, others will still appreciate your candor. They might agree or disagree with what you are saying but hey, you have accomplished your aim.

Saying Hello #10: *"Will it be alright if I join you here? I need a little quiet. This event has gone crazy."*

Saying Hello #11: *"Are you here with someone? My friend left me so I hope it would be okay if I keep you company."*

Saying Hello #12: *"Have you talked to anyone yet? Or am I your first just like you are mine?"*

Saying Hello #13: *"Is it quieter here? I could hardly hear my own voice over there."*

Look around. In any event, you will always find people who are on their own, just standing alone, and looking like they had like to be anywhere but there. You can walk up to them and introduce yourself. You will be doing them the favor because most likely, these people may just have had problems initiating conversations.

Saying Hello #14: *"Wow, I love your purse."*

Saying Hello #15: *"Your dress looks awesome!"*

This is an effective way to start especially for women. Just remember that you must mean what you say because other people are very skilled in knowing if you are being sincere just by looking at your facial expressions and non-verbal cues.

Giving out compliments will not only make you seem friendly, it will also create a light atmosphere conducive for a conversation. Just make sure you are true to your compliments. Otherwise, it would also connote negativity or sarcasm. You would not want to be told that you are wearing a really nice dress when you know it is not at all good and you have no choice for you have nothing else to wear for that particular occasion and you are having a very awkward feeling. Be sensitive though. If you see someone feeling uneasy, make sure you do not feed his or her uneasiness. Make him or her forget about it by giving that person some diversion.

Saying Hello #16: *"You are a fan of Miami Heat? Did you see their game yesterday?"*

Saying Hello #17: *"Did you, by any chance, catch the game last night? I missed it."*

Men are very welcome to try this way. Women, of course, can also opt to embrace this method. You just have to make sure that you can sustain the conversation that you'll initiate. Do not change the topic out of nowhere once you have started it just because you know nothing about sports, after all.

Your observation skills will come into play in this method. Notice if they are wearing a sports-related accessory and you can comment on that.

Saying Hello #18: *"Hey, since we are still waiting, we might as well talk."*

Saying Hello #19: *"This line is so long. I wonder what time we get to let go of it."*

If you ever find yourself in a place where people are congregating, don't let the opportunity pass. Say, you're in the bathroom and women are lining up. Take the chance and talk to those in front of you.

Saying Hello #20: *"What brought you here today?"*

Saying Hello #21: *"What do you do?"*

Saying Hello #22: *"How did you hear about this event?"*

Saying Hello #23: *"Hey, have you been here long?"*

Saying Hello #24: *"Is this your first time at this kind of event?"*

Saying Hello #25: *"Are you a member of X organization?"*

Instead of segueing to other topics, you can always go straight to asking people about their jobs or what brought them to the event. Some people actually appreciate straight talkers. Asking them something personal – but please, not too much – will make them open up about themselves and will keep the conversation flowing.

Saying Hello #26: *"Are you here alone, or do you know anyone else here?"*

This is a good way of knowing if there are other people that you can add to your contacts. If you ever meet someone who is with company, bring them into your circle. However, if they are also flying solo, you can immediately garner some sympathy for being alone there.

Saying Hello #27: *"Do you know a good tourist attraction here?"*

Saying Hello #28: *"Where are the best food places here?"*

If you know for sure that the person you plan to approach is a local, you can start your conversation by asking them about their place and perhaps the attractions it can offer. But if they are not, you can share ideas between the two of you regarding the places that you have heard are ideal for some sightseeing.

Saying Hello #29: *"What did you think about what X said?"*

Saying Hello #30: *"What a great speech, right? X has some great insights."*

You can also draw inspiration for conversation starters from the speeches or sessions that you went through with other people.

Saying Hello #31: *"Can I help you with that?"*

If you ever see someone struggling with their plate of food, the door, the chair, etc., you can approach them and give a hand and start a conversation afterwards.

Chapter 5 - 31 Ways To End Conversations

Conversation enders are important because they can help you secure the contact information of the person you have been talking to. When done correctly, people would be willing to keep in touch with you in the future. Make sure that you do not leave a bad taste in their mouths as you part ways after the event has ended or after your conversation has concluded.

Saying Goodbye #1: *"I'm going to get a refill for my cup. It was great meeting you!"*

Saying Goodbye #2: *"Look at that, I think it is past my bedtime already. I think I need to go. I would love for us to talk again. May I have your contact information?"*

Saying Goodbye #3: *"I can finally get some food since the line has died down. Talking to you was fun. Is there a way for us to keep in touch with each other?"*

Saying Goodbye #4: *"Thank you for your time but I just noticed that I am running late for my next appointment. It was nice meeting you."*

Saying Goodbye #5: *"I can finally get some food since the line has died down. Talking to you was fun. Is there a way for us to keep in touch with each other?"*

Saying Goodbye #6: *"Well, it is my first time here so I think I am going to say hello to a few more people. Thanks for your ideas. May I contact you in the future?"*

Saying Goodbye #7: *"I really enjoyed our conversation. I hope we get to have more."*

Saying Goodbye #8: *"I can finally get some food since the line has died down.*

Talking to you was fun. Is there a way for us to keep in touch with each other?"

Saying Goodbye #9: *"It was a fun night. See you around."*

Saying Goodbye #10: *"I enjoyed talking to you. Would you mind giving me your contact information?"*

Saying Goodbye #11: *"I can finally get some food since the line has died down. Talking to you was fun. Is there a way for us to keep in touch with each other?"*

Saying Goodbye #12: *"It is time for me to hit the loo. It was fun discussing with you."*

Saying Goodbye #13: *"I need to go first. I hope you enjoy the rest of your time here."*

Saying Goodbye #14: *"I'm going to check out the food bar. See you around!"*

Saying Goodbye #15: *"Hey, my friend wants to bounce some ideas with you. I'll just go and fill my stomach. Have fun!"*

Saying Goodbye #16: *"It's getting pretty late. I guess I'll get going, then."*

Saying Goodbye #17: *"Man, I'm beat. I need my bed. It was awesome meeting you. Would it be possible to keep in touch with you?"*

Saying Goodbye #18: *"We should talk again sometime after this event."*

Saying Goodbye #19: *"This has been really brilliant but I need to get going. Thank you for your company."*

Saying Goodbye #20: *"Thanks for bearing with me."*

Saying Goodbye #21: *"I have to be somewhere. I enjoyed talking to you, though. Maybe we can talk afterwards?"*

Saying Goodbye #22: *"Would you mind if I go? I think I saw someone I really need to talk to."*

Saying Goodbye #23: *"It's gotten crazy in there. I think I need to rest. Enjoy the rest of your night!"*

Saying Goodbye #24: *"I would love to pick your brain again. Would you mind if I ask for your contact information?"*

Saying Goodbye #25: *"I'll think about what you suggested. Thank you for your time."*

Saying Goodbye #26: *"I'm sorry. I need to go so I can still catch a cab. Spending time with you was worthwhile, so thank you."*

Saying Goodbye #27: *"I remembered that I have to run through some ideas with my colleague. I'll just go and talk to them. Thanks for the company."*

Saying Goodbye #28: *"I need some coffee. It was great talking to you."*

Saying Goodbye #29: *"It seems like I'm hogging all your time. See you around."*

Saying Goodbye #30: *"You have really interesting thoughts. I hope I get to talk to you again. Can I get your contact info?"*

Saying Goodbye #31: *"I had an awesome night. See you!"*

All these lines should suggest that you have enjoyed your talk and you are certainly looking forward to meeting that person again and the same should be felt by your recipient. Letting them know how great it was to talk with them make them feel good too. Not only is it a start to sealing that deal but a kick-start for your network expansion.

Chapter 6 - Keeping In Touch After Your First Meeting

Now that you have your database of contacts for your business network, do not let that simply sleep there. You have their contact information which you have collected with much effort so never put those to waste. Get the ball rolling and schedule that next possible meeting. You can identify these contacts in your network then and have a good segregation. These can be your potential clients, a group who can pave the way to more connections or partners as they have the means to find your possible customers or they can be influencers. Categories these contacts according to the degree in which they can be relevant to your business. Draw a huge loop and you can have an inner, middle and outer loop.

Keeping in touch with your circles or those that are in your network means not only meeting them face-to-face. Though it means a lot, there can be times when it would seem impossible. What should you do then? Do not disregard phone numbers. That is why you got their contact info so you can phone them! A personal note can likewise be of great help.

CONCLUSION

You have finally reached the last part of this book. I would like to congratulate you for having a good finish and at the same time, I would like to thank you again for downloading this book!

I hope this book was able to help you to understand what business networking is and its importance to you and your business. It is an avenue for career growth as you open yourself up to possible collaborations too in the future.

But it always starts with a good talk. You may have that enthusiasm in mind but that is easily burned down the moment you face your potentials. You get tongue stuck aside from having the unusual feeling of having butterflies in your stomach.

Then again, making conversations is one of the major tasks when you are involved in business networking. Knowing the right things to say to the right people at the right time would greatly help in making your endeavors succeed.

Starting your conversations appropriately will help in establishing connections with various people who will remember the impression you left when you were talking. It would also guarantee a more likely chance that they will keep in touch with you and entertain you in the future.

Likewise, ending a conversation on the right note will affect how many connections you can create and the quality of these relationships. If you come off as dismissive and offensive when you say goodbye, you might as well consider the contact information that you got as useless because it's possible that you'll get a less than lukewarm response from these people in case you approach them again.

The next step is to apply what you have learned from your readings here. Face the mirror, practice and you will be perfectly on your way to building a strong network with your potential members or partners. I wish you nothing but the best in all your endeavors then!

Finally, if you enjoyed this book, then I'd like to ask you for a favor, would you be kind enough to leave a review for this book on Amazon? It'd be greatly appreciated!

Click here to leave a review for this book on Amazon!

Thank you and good luck!